1/10

MILITARY HELICOPTERS

IN ACTION

Kay Jackson

PowerKiDS
press™

New York

To Carl and all the flight medics who risk their lives to save others

Published in 2009 by The Rosen Publishing Group, Inc.
29 East 21st Street, New York, NY 10010

First Edition

Editor: Nicole Pristash
Book Design: Julio Gil
Photo Researcher: Jessica Gerweck

Photo Credits: Cover, pp. 13, 14, 17 Courtesy of the Department of Defense; pp. 5, 6, 9, 18 © Getty Images; p. 10 Shutterstock.com; p. 21 © U.S. Air Force/Age Fotostock.

Library of Congress Cataloging-in-Publication Data

Jackson, Kay, 1959–
   Military helicopters in action / Kay Jackson. — 1st ed.
      p. cm. — (Amazing military vehicles)
   Includes index.
   ISBN 978-1-4358-2748-6 (library binding) — ISBN 978-1-4358-3158-2 (pbk.)
ISBN 978-1-4358-3164-3 (6-pack)
   1. Military helicopters—Juvenile literature. I. Title.
   UG1233.J33 2009
   623.74'6047—dc22

                                2008032445

Manufactured in the United States of America

CONTENTS

Helicopters Save Lives

A downed **pilot** hides in the woods and waits for help. A small Army base in the desert needs more earth-moving machines. On a high mountain, a hurt soldier is ready for an airlift. In the Pacific Ocean, a fishing-boat captain reports that his boat is sinking.

What ties all these things together? Military helicopters do. Helicopters will be used to find the pilot, move the machines, carry the soldier to a hospital, and save the captain and his crew. These are just a few of the jobs done every day by the military helicopters of the United States.

This U.S. Navy helicopter is searching for people caught in the floodwaters caused by Hurricane Katrina in 2005.

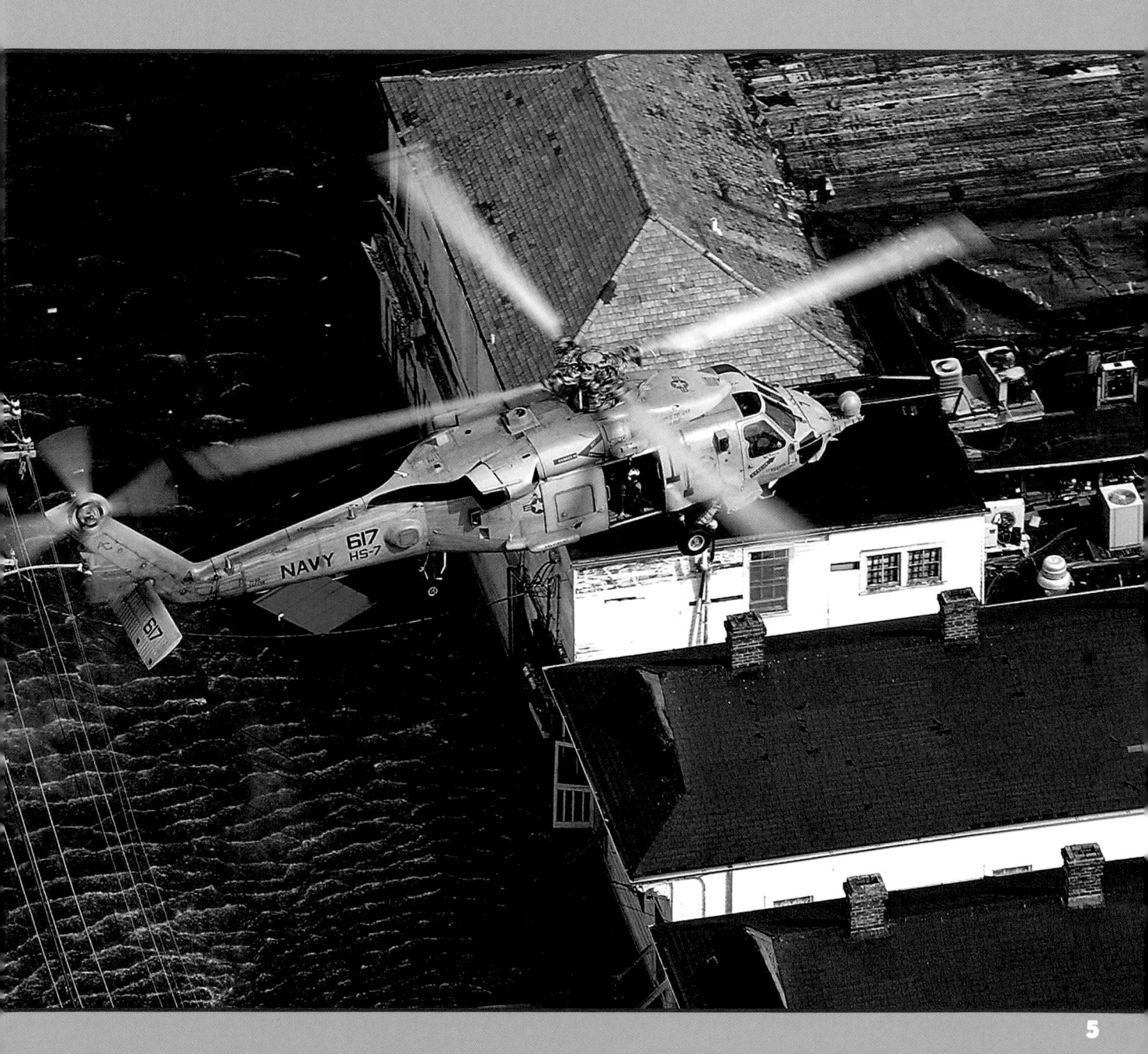

The Bell UH-1 Iroquois, shown here, was a popular U.S. helicopter used during the Vietnam War in the 1960s and 1970s. Its nickname is the Huey.

Helicopters in War

U.S. military helicopters were first used in World War II. They were small and they had open cockpits. In the 1950s, helicopters were used mainly to move hurt soldiers and tools. However, that changed in the 1960s.

The helicopter found its place in the U.S. military during the Vietnam War. The military had large **cargo** helicopters, but it needed a helicopter to go deep behind enemy lines. By the early 1970s, the military's first true attack helicopter was flying. It carried **missiles** and powerful machine guns. Today, helicopters take on some of the most important jobs in the military.

Flying Without Wings

Helicopters are rotary aircraft. This means that they do not have fixed wings, as planes do. Instead, helicopters have long blades that are attached to a **rotor**. The rotor spins, and the blades push air down, creating **lift**.

Military helicopters are built to be strong. Some have special **tanks**. If **bullets** make holes in these tanks, the holes seal over. Many military helicopters also have Forward-Looking **Infrared Radar**, or FLIR. FLIR picks up heat. It lets a pilot see a person's body heat or hot engine parts at night. Military helicopters also carry missiles to fire at the enemy.

Here a marine is checking the rotor of a CH-53 Sea Stallion cargo helicopter. A marine is a member of the Marines, a branch of the U.S. military.

This rescue swimmer is jumping into the ocean from a Coast Guard helicopter. Rescue swimmers know how to jump safely so they can save people quickly.

3 1833 05800 3945

Who Uses Helicopters?

Every branch of the U.S. military uses helicopters. The Air Force uses helicopters to find downed pilots. The Coast Guard uses helicopters to **rescue** people lost or hurt at sea. Navy helicopters move cargo every day. The Marines move their tools and fighting teams with helicopters. However, the Army uses helicopters the most.

Army helicopters fly ground troops to camps near enemy lines. They carry special teams that slide down a rope 60 feet (18 m) above the ground. Army helicopters pick up and move military cars and trucks from one base to another. Helicopters are used for fighting, too.

Attack Helicopters

By flying low, a pilot in an attack helicopter can spot an enemy convoy. A convoy is a line of trucks. The helicopter fires missiles at the convoy. Then, guns on the helicopter's nose fire on the trucks. Attack helicopters also fly above their own troops, keeping them safe.

The AH-64D Apache Longbow is the Army's fastest attack helicopter. Some people think it is the world's most dangerous attack helicopter. The Apache looks different from other helicopters. It is thin and fits two people. Its short wings carry missiles. Infrared sensors help the crew find the enemy at night.

The AH-64D Apache Longbow is the most advanced helicopter used today. In 30 seconds, this helicopter can find enemy forces and fire on them.

These Navy men are using the Army's UH-60 Blackhawk helicopter for training. The group is practicing ways to move wounded people quickly.

A Helicopter with Many Jobs

Utility helicopters can do many jobs in the military. A utility helicopter might carry people one day. The next day, it could be taking hundreds of bottles of water to thirsty soldiers.

One of the world's most useful utility helicopters is the Army's UH-60 Blackhawk. With boxes of food inside, the Blackhawk is a cargo helicopter. If doctors and their tools are on board, the Blackhawk becomes a flying hospital. A team of soldiers and their packs turns the Blackhawk into a troop carrier. When missiles are put on it, the Blackhawk becomes a fighting helicopter.

Moving the Military

When the military needs heavy lifting done, it uses a cargo helicopter. Cargo helicopters can pick up trucks, bulldozers, and even small jets. These helicopters fly thousands of pounds (kg) of food, bullets, computers, cars, tools, or whatever else the military needs moved.

One of the biggest cargo helicopters is the CH-53E Super Stallion. The Super Stallion's main rotor blades are 79 feet (24 m) across! The Navy and the Marines use the Super Stallion all over the world. The Super Stallion can fly cargo over mountains, across the icy Arctic, or through the blazing hot desert.

The CH-53E Super Stallion has three engines, and it can lift 16 tons (14.5 t). Here it is shown during a Marine training exercise in Arizona.

This Coast Guard member is lowering a metal basket out of the HH-65 Dolphin helicopter. The metal basket is used to carry people out of the water.

Finding the Hurt and Lost

When people, planes, or boats are lost, search and rescue helicopters are sent out. These small, light helicopters often carry special rescue tools, such as metal baskets. A rope is used to lower the basket. Then, a hurt person is put in the basket and brought up to the rescue helicopter.

The U.S. Coast Guard uses the HH-65 Dolphin. The Dolphin was made to make search and rescue easier. It can stay above a boat without drifting away. Also, the Dolphin's computers can make it fly a pattern over the water. This helps the pilot search for the lost.

Helicopter Crews

Military helicopters are flown by a crew. An attack helicopter can have a pilot and a copilot. Utility and cargo helicopters may have four to six people in a crew.

One crew member is the crew chief. The chief makes sure everything is working and watches over the loading and unloading of the helicopter. Another crew member is the gunner. The gunner fires at the enemy forces to keep them away. The pilot leads the helicopter crew. The pilot plans the day's job and trains crew members. She checks the weather and makes sure the right tools are on the helicopter.

This pilot is flying a HH-60 Pave Hawk helicopter. The helicopter is refueling a C-130 plane in midair. Fuel is what powers helicopters and planes.

Tomorrow's Helicopters

Military helicopters are becoming more interesting and special. The CV-22 Osprey is one of those special helicopters. The Osprey takes off and lands like a helicopter. It lands in small, tight places like fields or boat decks. However, when the Osprey is in the air, it can turn its **propellers** forward. Then, the Osprey can fly fast like a plane.

Today's military helicopters can do many things. They can lift big loads or fight off the enemy. Tomorrow's helicopters will have many new jobs. Military helicopters will continue to change to fit these important jobs for a long time to come.

Glossary

bullets (BU-lets) Things that are shot out of a gun.

cargo (KAHR-goh) The load of goods carried by an airplane, a ship, a helicopter, or a car.

infrared (in-fruh-RED) Light waves that are outside of the part of the light range at the red end, which we can see.

lift (LIFT) The force of air on a helicopter's blades that makes the helicopter fly.

missiles (MIH-sulz) Objects that are shot at something far away in order to hurt or kill.

pilot (PY-lut) A person who flies an aircraft.

propellers (pruh-PEL-erz) Paddlelike parts on an object that spin to move the object forward.

radar (RAY-dahr) A machine that uses sound waves or radio waves to find objects.

rescue (RES-kyoo) To save someone or something from danger.

rotor (ROH-ter) A machine that makes power by turning or spinning.

tanks (TANGKS) Large objects for holding water or other matter.

utility (yoo-TIH-luh-tee) Usefulness.

Index

B
base, 4, 11
boat(s), 4, 19

C
Coast Guard, 11, 19
crew, 4, 12, 20

D
desert, 4, 16

F
Forward-Looking
    Infrared Radar
    (FLIR), 8

H
hospital, 4, 15

L
line(s), 7, 11–12

M
missiles, 7–8, 12, 15
mountain(s), 4, 16

P
Pacific Ocean, 4
pilot(s), 4, 8, 11–12,
    19–20
propellers, 22

R
rotor, 8

S
soldier(s), 4, 7, 15

T
tanks, 8

U
United States, 4

W
woods, 4

Web Sites

Due to the changing nature of Internet links, PowerKids Press has developed an online list of Web sites related to the subject of this book. This site is updated regularly. Please use this link to access the list:

www.powerkidslinks.com/amv/copters/